A Gent Guide to Women, Commoners & Cooking

Compiled by Little Biographies

Edited by Jonathan Diack

First published in 2020 by
Little Biographies

Second edition published in 2021 by
Old English Press

Editor's Note

This guide presumes to instruct the reader in the process of selecting a bride, dealing with commoners and preparing food. Gentlemen are normally fed by others. Thus it may be argued that instructions on cooking are superfluous. From time to time however gentlemen are subject to indiscretion. The third part of the guide anticipates the unfortunate yet almost inevitable situation when the reader strays sufficiently from the straight and narrow path to bring upon himself the absence, temporary or permanent, of his wife and kitchen staff.

The guide also serves to provide commoners with an insight into the life of twenty-first century gentlemen. The suffocating gloom imposed upon the general public by virtue of woke-minded liberal and socialist ideologies has yet to permeate the manor houses and great estates of the country, most of which continue to be alive with the gaiety and unparalleled eccentricity for which the British upper classes have long been renowned.

Part 1

A Gentleman's Guide to Women

Introduction

Men gave up trying to understand women a long time ago, and rightly so. The priorities are different. A well bred male will ride his estate in the morning, jumping a few fences and hedges to keep in trim for the foxhunting season, acknowledging along the way the doffed caps of the local peasantry. In the afternoon he will stroll to the river with a favourite rod, or take his dogs and a gun to a shaded copse, from where he will emerge later to dine and drink extravagantly before stumbling into bed at midnight to pleasure whomsoever happens to be lying between the sheets.

Meanwhile his wife will have spent the day organising the domestic staff, looking after the household accounts, mustering the gardeners, planning menus, monitoring children, arranging flowers in the great hall, decorating the church, attending the parish council meeting, visiting the baker's wife who has shingles, dealing with telephone calls and eventually, exhausted, making sure she is the one lying between the sheets when her husband stumbles into bed.

In this manner reigns marital bliss until a suave Italian count persuades your wife that she is being taken for granted and lures her from your estate to a life in luxury in Portofino, eating grapes on the balcony of an extensive villa overlooking the deep blue sea from where she sends you rude postcards.

The purpose of the first part of this publication is to instruct you on those essential aspects of women, the knowledge of which will enable you pursue your interests uninterrupted by anxiety that your beautiful companion might suddenly disappear leaving you obliged, amongst other inconveniences, to attend parish council meetings.

Contents

Early Encounters

How not to impress girls - 1

The parents are hacking ahead. You and Ophelia are trying to keep pace. Ophelia's pony shies suddenly at a weasel on the dry stone wall lining the track, tossing her onto the ground where she lies white-faced, one leg twisted at an unnatural angle. You shout to the parents, dismount and attend to Ophelia who by now has passed out. The parents gallop back. You are complimented on your quick response to the incident although in truth you did nothing particularly special. Nonetheless the compliments continue and you bask modestly in your role as a heroic figure until luncheon the following day when your mother suggests you visit the local hospital to see Ophelia whose leg has been set and lies homesick in the ward.

It is well known that boys dislike hospitals as much as they dislike the embarrassment of forced encounters with girls but you have no choice in the matter. Miserably that afternoon you embark upon the mission.

'I've brought you a present,' you say, standing awkwardly at Ophelia's bedside.

'How absolutely sweet of you. What is it?'

'A shotgun cartridge.'

'Oh,' says Ophelia cautiously. 'Is it live?'

'Yes. When you drop it, it makes a terrific noise,' you say, dropping the cartridge onto the floor as Ophelia and the other patients in the ward dive under their sheets.

Saddling up for a ride with Ophelia

How not to impress girls - 2

You are now thirteen. Ophelia's father is visiting the estate bringing Ophelia with him, who wanders around the library, bored. You observe her from the door. She glances in your direction, eyes mischievously half-concealed behind her fingers. She beckons you.

'What's up?' you say shuffling towards her.

'Why don't we go and play croquet, it's a lovely day?' she says.

'I'm afraid that's impossible.'

'Why?' she enquires.

'I've taken a vow of chastity.'

The sound of her muffled laughter accompanies your departure as you shuffle back to the door.

Analysis

Encounter 1

Boys enjoy storing articles like shotgun cartridges in their beds, girls don't. What's more, you know perfectly well that cartridges don't explode on mere contact with the floor. You were showing off, demonstrating your mastery of events, whereas you should of course have presented Ophelia with a bunch of flowers plucked on your way through the meadow.

Encounter 2

By now you are fascinated by the alluring aspect of girls and would rather liked to have played croquet with Ophelia. But, wary of being thought soppy and instinctively determined to exert mastery, you attempt one of those droll remarks that drip effortlessly from the lips of grown-ups. Girls are much shrewder than boys. Ophelia has no problem understanding the basis for your ridiculous remark. You should have offered your arm and said 'With great pleasure.'

3

Growing Frustration

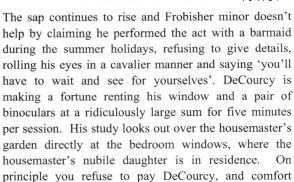

The sap continues to rise and Frobisher minor doesn't help by claiming he performed the act with a barmaid during the summer holidays, refusing to give details, rolling his eyes in a cavalier manner and saying 'you'll have to wait and see for yourselves'. DeCourcy is making a fortune renting his window and a pair of binoculars at a ridiculously large sum for five minutes per session. His study looks out over the housemaster's garden directly at the bedroom windows, where the housemaster's nubile daughter is in residence. On principle you refuse to pay DeCourcy, and comfort yourself with the certainty that Frobisher minor is lying.

'Have you paid DeCourcy for a look yet ?'

The Art of Small Talk

Seasonal dances provide the opportunity of mingling with girls without fear of ridicule. See if you can work out which of the following attempts at light conversation is most likely to lead to a goodnight kiss later.

Example - 1

'Catching the mongoose, that's the problem, you see,' you say leading your partner to the floor.

'Really,' she says.

'And stuffing it afterwards,' you continue setting off for the waltz, arm around her waist.

'Is that so?'

'We've got one at home, mounted above the fireplace in the great hall. The trouble is, its tail dangles down.'

'Fancy.'

'And gets singed by the flames.'

'It must do.'

'Which creates an awful stink.'

'Oh dear.'

'Still, on the bright side, the smell drives the rats out of the bell tower.'

Example - 2

'I can't believe my luck, dancing with someone so lovely,' you say leading your partner to the floor.

'Flatterer!'

'I was quite overwhelmed when I saw you across the room.'

'Nonsense,' your partner protests sweetly.

'Do you mind me asking, is your dress made by Chanel in Paris?'

'Not exactly.'

'How modest. The last time I saw such an elegant dress was at a film festival, worn by that famous young actress, I've forgotten her name. Although, if you don't mind me saying, the design looks far more beautiful on you.'

5

Fulfilment

Your seventeenth birthday is spent on a yacht engaged by your father to cruise the Greek islands. Amongst the guests onboard is a rich French art dealer and his daughter, Jacqueline, slightly older than you, sensuously proportioned and exuding enough pheromones to start a Trojan war. Your efforts to impress her with your masculine physique, your skill at double-somersaults from the side of the yacht into the blue Mediterranean and standing on your head while water skiing have transparently failed to impress her even less than your attempts at luncheon to quantify Flaubert's influence on European literature, your voice tailing off when you realised you were confusing Flaubert with Balzac. Never mind. The celestial powers are about to take pity on your plight.

Pheromone dispenser

Forbidden fruit

Shortly after midnight, according to the clock beside your bunk, you hear a knock on the door. You open it to find Jacqueline standing in the passageway wearing a provocatively short nightdress. She is holding an apple, which she offers you. 'Thank you,' you say closing the door and returning to your bunk with the apple, surprised but gratified at the gift though confused by the timing. You are dropping off to sleep again when you jack-knife up in bed, cuff your head, grab your dressing gown and rush down the passageway to Jacqueline's cabin where you are received with perfumed passion and where, next morning, you awake proudly to manhood.

Your father has rented a yacht for the summer

Gallant Soldier

You have been accepted into a fashionable regiment, more on the basis that the colonel is your godfather and that you are a reasonable shot on the grouse moors than evidence of military acumen. Swaggering from St James's Palace in your dashingly elegant uniform you are conscious of receiving attention from the well-groomed girls on shopping breaks from Christie's. You do not respond to their glances however. There are more important things on your mind. Now that you have been inducted into the hall of manhood there is no point in wasting time on bouts of trivial conversation with girls of your own background who in a hundred years would not be seen dead standing half naked in the middle of the night between decks of a yacht handing out apples to members of the opposite sex.

The assumption that well-bred girls are above horseplay is, of course, incorrect. Almost as incorrect as the belief that you now know everything a man could possibly need to know about women when in fact your experience is limited to the knowledge that double-somersaults into the Mediterranean and the ability to water ski upside down can result in spasmodic episodes of sublime pleasure.

You have tasted the forbidden fruit and understandably want more. Fortuitously your regimental duties allow you plenty of time for nights at an establishment in Mayfair, the lush epitome of private dining where, after the tables are cleared, the diners enjoy entertainment from scantily-clad young ladies with sympathetic views of carnality. The establishment is expensive however. 'Can you explain this account I have received from Oodles Dining Club in London for £22,050 for services rendered?' says your father one weekend, eyebrows raised.

Somehow you manage to convince your father that Oodles is an exclusive hat shop where you got carried away purchasing an expensive arrangement of peacock feathers for your aunt's birthday. Time is running out however and you are about to make a terrible mistake.

Terrible Mistake - 1

'Bubbles, darling,' you say clearing your throat during a break between shows.

'Yes, my gallant soldier,' says the girl on your lap feeding you pieces of chocolate truffle.

'You know the diamond necklace I bought you?'

'Know it?! I worship it. It's the greatest gift this girl ever received. Why do you ask, my gallant soldier?'

'The fact is I'm a bit short at the moment, my allowance is running out, well, you see, I wonder if we could treat the necklace as a loan . . . ?'

'Loan?'

There is a sharp intake of breath. The delivery of chocolate truffle ceases and the subsequent altercation attracts the attention of the club's security staff. Next morning you are invited to explain to your adjutant the reason for the scratches on your face.

Takes a sympathetic view of carnality,
up to a point

A far cry from Oodles Dining Club

Rehabilitation

The unfortunate incident at the club in London has forced a change of circumstances. You are now at Oxford, less for your academic accomplishments at school, described by your housemaster as elusive, than for the happy coincidence that your great uncle Percival is an important figure at one of the great mediaeval colleges, with willow trees lining the banks of the Cherwell.

Your uncle makes some helpful suggestions on the matter of how to conduct yourself at college, urging you to involve yourself in healthy sporting and social activities, control your alcohol intake and avoid being distracted by over-frequent involvement with the opposite sex. I shall watch your progress with interest, says your uncle ushering you from his chambers in a manner so courteous and affectionate it belies the probability he has already arranged for your movements on and off the campus to be closely monitored. To make matters worse, your father has taken revenge on your far-fetched feather hat invention by trimming your allowance.

You apply to train for the college rowing team. You picture yourself gliding effortlessly down the river, the blade of your oar gleaming in the sunlight at the precise angle prescribed by the legendary coxswains whose names adorn

Harder than it looks

the boathouse walls and receive a nasty shock at the amount of physical discomfort the coach expects you to endure. When the blisters on your hands have healed sufficiently you transfer to the tennis team being careful, in view of the ongoing surveillance programme, to avoid mixed doubles.

Academically you select the Greek gods as your principal subject of study and surprise your tutor by submitting a lucid paper on the role of Heracles within the Dorian lineage. Your tutor informs your uncle that you appear to be settling down. Your uncle conveys the information to your father. Nodding approvingly the persons most closely responsible for your welfare could be forgiven for concluding you were on the road to recovery and had come to understand the importance of rejecting the temptations of the flesh. How misguided of them.

Heracles by Canova, as referenced in your paper

Irresistible Cleavage

Your downfall at Oxford begins when you are invited to play an upper class scoundrel in an amusing new production of *'Springtime Sneezes'* by one of the university's theatrical groups. You protest your lack of stage experience but the director, desperate to find someone sufficiently debonair for the part, pounces on you at a party in Summertown. Simply be yourself, he cries. Flattered and amused by the invitation, which presents an admirable opportunity of demonstrating to your uncle your commitment to healthy social activities, you accept. Your leading lady is not so enthusiastic about your lack of acting experience however and treats you coolly. Attractive and well built, she is renowned for outbursts of temperament. Fortunately you are not required to kiss her, only to rip the necklace from her throat crying 'If I cannot possess you, these pearls are mine!' in a scene eerily reminiscent of your downfall in London.

Adept at playing the fool you discover an aptitude for acting. The director compliments you on your timing. In the scene when the butler bursts onto the stage crying 'The ballroom is on fire, my lord!', your drawled response 'Well don't stand there, Jenkins, go and warm yourself' brings the house down. The theatre is full every night, and the critics are complimentary.

In retrospect it was a mistake on the last night of the production to consume so much champagne during the interval. The audience rocked with laughter as you reeled towards the leading lady in the 'these pearls are mine' scene. The longer you stood in front of her, swaying unsteadily, the more they laughed until, reaching forward with the sweeping motion of your hand intended to dislodge the pearls, you removed the front of her dress. Bare-breasted and wailing the leading lady fled the stage.

Next day you write a note of apology, conveying deep regrets at the embarrassment you caused and expressing relief that the situation had not been worse. At least you were spared the ordeal of having your dress completely ripped off, you write, and thank heavens nobody took a photograph. A picture on the front page of The Sunday Times, for example, you continue, would have worsened the offense intolerably. Tucking the envelope into an expensive bouquet of flowers you proceed to the red brick building in North Oxford where the star of the show lives. You knock on the door rehearsing your speech. There is no answer. A window opens above your head. You look up in time to see a plastic bowl emerging. The cascade of lukewarm water, bacon rinds and associated items of kitchen waste catches you full in the face. Wiping the debris from your ensemble you return to your motor vehicle. 'All square, I suppose,' you mutter, starting the engine.

Hell hath no fury like a woman exposed upon the stage

Analysis

1. By now you have learned that women are more than just languorous purveyors of passion. In adverse circumstances they can be venemous.

2. You should have made more effort with the leading lady. It is quite possible her coolness towards you masked caution at dealing with someone so flamboyantly priviliged.

3. Your note of apology was deficient. It is small comfort for a lady to be informed that her breasts have not featured on the front page of *The Sunday Times*.

4. The possibility exists that you removed her bodice deliberately, in which case the lesson is that women normally get the last laugh, witness the bacon rinds on your face.

Out of your Depth

Under increased supervision from your uncle you withdraw even further from the social scene in Oxford and concentrate on your books. During the course of your studies you meet a bright girl called Felicity who is taking a degree in linguistics with special interest in the classical period of Mediterranean history. You share the same period of study, albeit approaching ancient Greece from a different direction. She infects you with such enthusiasm for her field that you alter your approach to your own subject in a manner that will eventually earn you a second in the Greats and go some way to redeeming your reputation.

Her academic range is wider than yours. You take pleasure in testing her opinions, and enjoy her company enough to spend your diminished allowance on punting excursions on the Cherwell and modestly priced meals at waterside inns. She is from ordinary stock, wears glasses and is not particularly beautiful. She is flattered by the attentions of someone so cosmopolitan and grand as yourself, and calls you Croesus, after the wealthy king.

'Do you really have servants at home?' she asks.

'Yes.'

'How many?'

'I don't know.'

'What do you mean, you don't know?'

Punting on the Cherwell

'I've never counted.'

'Presumably somebody has?'

She is careful not to overpower you intellectually, nor to respond impatiently when you lose track of her arguments. You begin to rely on her company, to assume that she will always answer your telephone calls and be available for dinner. So it comes as a shock when she starts to put your calls on hold. More so when one afternoon you see her crossing the quadrangle conversing animatedly with another male undergraduate. 'I'm sorry, Croesus, it's time for me to move on,' she informs you gently.

Terrible Mistake - 2

Hurt beyond measure you sleep badly, tossing and turning in bed, hammering the pillows. Life without Felicity is too dreadful to contemplate, you tell yourself. You buy a ring and propose to her kneeling on the floor of the King's Arms. She declines sweetly, vowing to treasure the memories of your times together, declaring she will always be your friend etc. Rubbing salt into the wound the jeweller refuses to take the ring back.

'It's out of fashion, I'm afraid'.

'I only bought it yesterday,' you complain.

'*Tempus fugit*, as they say,' says the man sucking his teeth.

You return to your rooms, toss the ring out of the window and sink morbidly into an armchair.

Review

1. Whew, that was close! You were way out of your depth with Felicity.

2. For a relationship to succeed the woman should be as clever as the man, if not cleverer, but not to the extent that by comparison the man is dumb.

3. Moreover Felicity was not equipped to become the mistress of a large estate and would have floundered in the grandeur of the local hunt ball.

4. Let's face it, the last thing you want at this stage of your life is a wife, just someone to help with your thesis.

15

Oriental  Interlude

Your uncle unwisely asks you to look after a Korean girl arriving to take a degree course in English. Her wealthy father has indicated he will make a significant donation to the college if she settles down happily and completes the course. 'Don't touch her,' warns your uncle. 'Of course not,' you sniff, visualising a peasant girl with puffed-up face and slanting eyes. You stand on the platform at Oxford railway station holding a placard with her name painted in Korean script searching for passengers wearing conical bamboo hats when you are approached by a beautiful girl with long legs and an engaging smile.

She points at the placard, nods and thumbs through a phrasebook. 'My many suitcase needs portering,' she says. 'Leave it to me,' you say gulping at your good fortune. She follows you to the car park and stares puzzled at your sleek open-top motor car, trying to place you within the university hierarchy. 'Me undergraduate,' you say. 'Me undergarment too,' she replies, consulting the dictionary section of her phrasebook.

Despite the language difficulty, you get along splendidly. You escort her around the university and show her the sights of Oxford, strolling through the botanical gardens, drinking at the Trout Inn and dining in the Randolph Hotel. Laughing happily at your inability to understand each other you make constant references to your respective dictionaries. Exactly twelve hours from the time of her arrival at the railway station you are romping together in bed.

On the third morning she announces she loves you. Your jaw drops. By now you are exhausted by the challenge of conducting a relationship via phrasebooks and dictionaries. You have a thesis to complete and badly need some sleep.

Your alarm is compounded when her father arrives to inspect the college. Burly, unsmiling and obviously dangerous he explains, with the use of illustrations of Korean ceremonial swords, what happens to persons who bring unhappiness to his daughter. Your uncle is unsympathetic and angry at the prospective loss of the endowment. 'I told you not to touch her!' he exclaims. He is also resourceful and arranges for you to be transferred to Yale University on a temporary exchange. By the time you return your beautiful Korean playmate has fallen for a French undergraduate studying oriental languages.

RULES OF CONDUCT
1

Take care before entering a relationship with a lady whose vocabulary in English is insufficient to debate Newton's third law of motion

Estate Management

Restored to grace by virtue of your degree in classical literature you move to Cirencester to study the principles of estate management and thereby complete your formal education. Joyfully you arrive sounding the horn of your open-top motor vehicle to be greeted by innumerable friends and acquaintances from your own background, sons and daughters of the hunting field, grouse moors and chalk streams. Allowance reinstated, you rent a picturesque wisteria-fronted cottage and renew your membership of the polo club.

There you meet the sister of a low-goal Argentinean instructor. You make an attractive couple, popular at parties and regular guests at smart events. She speaks English well, rides you off the ball fearlessly and is correspondingly vivacious between the sheets with no sign of the drama about to unfold.

Your handsome countenance and dashing demeanor naturally attract the attention of the other young females gathered at this centre of English agricultural excellence. Skilled in the subtle arts of allure they are constantly bumping into you with their soft curves, swathing you in subtle scents and fluttering their long eyelashes as they glide seductively past you in the corridor. A man can endure only so much temptation. In your case the threshold level is not high and one afternoon you yield to the inducements of a hazel-eyed veterinary student. You reel back afterwards to your cottage full of champagne. You attempt unsuccessfully to re-button your shirt and trousers as you stumble along the garden path. You open the door, spread your arms wide, shout 'Guess who?' and are felled by an ornamental vase. Your Argentinean girlfriend - by now in residence - has been waiting for you, tapping her foot angrily on the flagstone floor. Unsympathetically she helps you to the sofa.

'Dozens of them,' you groan.

'Of what?' she snaps, wiping the blood from your head.

'Maybe not a dozen, at least three.'

'Three what?'

'The attackers. I did my best, but there were too many. Just look what they did,' you groan in a forlorn attempt to explain the unbuttoned condition of your clothing.

Silently she returns to the sofa with a first aid box.

'What's the world coming to when you can't walk home without your clothes being ripped off?' you continue.

'How many of the attackers were wearing lipstick?' your Argentinean girlfriend enquires coolly.

'Eh?'

'Your face and shirt are covered in blush pink *L'Oréal*,' she says applying a plaster to the gash on your forehead.

Guiltily you squirm on the sofa.

'You are so lucky it was a vase not a knife,' she says, running up the stairs to the bedroom, slamming the door and locking it.

Next morning you assume an air of deep penitence but the spell is broken. Suitcase packed, she slaps you ceremonially across the face and moves out.

"Well, what was I supposed to do?"

RULES OF CONDUCT

2

If inclined to acts of indiscretion you should give ladies of volatile temperament a miss

The Root of the Problem

*'Daddy says I shall always
look beautiful'*

It is time to take stock of your position with the opposite sex. Quite rightly you understand that women do not stay beautiful for ever, despite the promises from their fathers The parade of lovely faces and voluptuous bodies which have enhanced your life as a young officer and undergraduate will be exchanged in matrimony for one young lady whose beauty will inevitably and steadily, and with increasing velocity, decline. Moreover the male comes to maturity later than the female (see graphs on opposite page). While the wife attempts to stem the tide of the ageing process with expensive ointments and surgical procedures the husband struts the stage like a peacock - handsome confident, tail feathers spread magnificently.

That is not the worst of it. Evidence points conclusively to the fact that men are not naturally monogamous. Programmed by his genes and given the opportunity the average male will attempt to fertilize anything wiggling attractively across his path.   When the pleasures of the marriage bed decline, which commonly occurs within one to seven years, is it any wonder that the male, now in his prime, strays from his marital vows?   Or that the female, anxious to verify that she is still sexually attractive, strays from hers?   Under the circumstances it is a miracle the institution of marriage has survived at all.

What then is the secret of successful union?

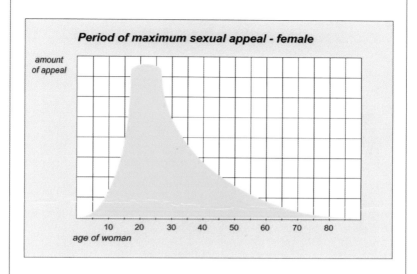

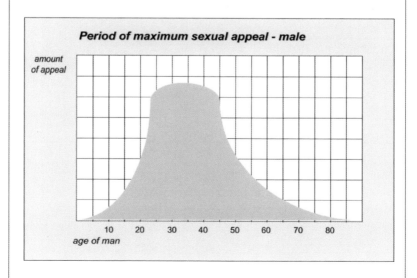

Temperament

The girl from the theatrical agency

Setting the scene

How will she react to indiscretion ?

While grappling with the problem of ageing, you might as well eliminate the most obvious risk to a fruitful relationship by establishing what may be described as the explosion point of your prospective bride. In the event that circumstances should arise during your time together whereby you commit one of more indiscretions then you don't want any more of those ornamental vases flying across the room, thank you very much.

By definition a gentleman is of sanguine disposition, ill-disposed towards turbulent behaviour during periods of sobriety, except when participating in field sports and subsequently, after consumption of wine, disinclined to participate in anything more boisterous than eightsome reels and the debagging of guests. So unless there is Latin blood in your veins, passed down through your mother's line and accustoming you to outbursts of temperament, prudence dictates that you select a bride capable of maintaining appropriate levels of sanguinity when, for example, you stumble home late at night and attempt to gain entry to the house by the main chimney stack.

Here is a simple test. Arrange with your local theatrical or escort agency for a provocatively dressed young woman to burst into your residence while you are dining with your prospective bride and kiss you passionately crying "I can't live without you, big boy!" Between the time the young woman departs and returns five minutes later to apologize for delivering the kissogram to the wrong address you should maintain an attitude of bemused innocence, occasionally flapping your hands muttering 'damnably odd' whilst carefully observing your prospective bride's reaction.

It is probably wise, in view of previous experience, to keep kitchen knives locked up during the period of the test.

The Half + Five Rule

Returning to the problem of ageing, a solution long-favoured by monarchs and tycoons is to take a young wife, an option readily available to gentlemen of means, and with numerous arguments in its favour.

The advantages to the female of an older husband are manifold. Under his protection she enjoys comfort and security and, in his eyes, her bloom scarcely fades. To the older man she is always beautiful, substantially reducing the likelihood that he will stray. For the rest of her life she bathes in the adoration of a faithful consort.

The advantages to a gentleman of a young bride are equally great. He acquires a playful companion for his bed and a home full of youthful laughter. Along the way he satisfies man's innate desire to possess beautiful objects. He becomes an art collector, possessing the finest prize of all. Indeed it can be argued that to see a silver-haired husband with a contented young wife on his arm is to enjoy a life-size portrait of human relationship at its most sublime.

Most experts recommend the half + five rule, in which the man's age is divided in half and five years added, to determine the optimum balance between the ages of the partners. Applying the calculation, a forty year old man should take a twenty five year old bride, and so on.

Proponents of the rule assert that the older you are, the greater the efficacy of the formula. Plunge into matrimony too young, they point out, and the gap between you and your bride will almost certainly be insufficient to mitigate the problem of ageing. So tally ho, they urge, sow your wild oats in your twenties and wait until the mantle of responsibility settles irrevocably upon your shoulders before selecting a lifetime companion.

Sow your wild oats in your twenties

Origins of the half+five rule

The first recorded reference to the formula now known as the half+five rule is to be found in the minutes of a meeting at the Rangoon Polo Club in August 1876. Major 'Stumpy' Carew proposed that to improve the quality of females in the club, most of whom he referred to as dross baggage, membership of the club should be restricted to officers and gentlemen whose wives were half their age, give or take five years. The major's name is missing from subsequent minutes. We may assume that senior members of the committee, whose wives had seen better days and qualified for the description of dross baggage, forced his resignation.

Shortly afterwards Major Carew turns up in Bombay. The social diary in the Times of India records several events which he attended accompanied by his 'lovely wife Angela'. From the photograph of Mrs Carew in 1885 reproduced below it may be deduced that the major practiced what he preached.

Trophy Shield, Rangoon Polo Club 1860

Angela Carew, Chelsea, 1885, posing for early colour photograph

Alternative Option

Alternatively you can turn the argument on its head and conclude that beauty is an overrated virtue, what matters is the magnetism of your bride's personality. Who cares about beauty if you are drawn to her laughter like a moth to a flame? Pursue this line of thought and you can extend your search for a bride into the extensive realm of older women.

Before hurtling off in that direction, however, be sure to establish what exactly she is laughing at. Remember that incident in the Savoy last year?

You were foraging amongst the cucumber sandwich at teatime when she swept past with her entourage and settled at a nearby table. Your eyes met, electricity flashed and before you could say 'Sorry, what a pity, I'm due back in Cirencester tomorrow' you were on the way to the Cannes film festival, sharing her bedroom and mixing with the stars. From Cannes the whirlwind romance continued to Hollywood, where you stayed in the Beverley Hills Hotel and overheard the following conversation between her and the head of Universal Studios.

'He's simply divine, darling, so British, so attentive. He's studying agriculture apparently. Between ourselves, darling, I don't think he knows the difference between a duck and a sheep, he's not the brightest, if you know what I mean, but gorgeously handsome and so much cheaper than renting from an agency.'

Whereupon you wrote a bill for your services as gigolo, removed a diamond bracelet from her dresser as collateral against payment and flew back to England.

Be sure to establish what exactly she is laughing at . . .

"I draw your attention to the seventh commandment . . ."

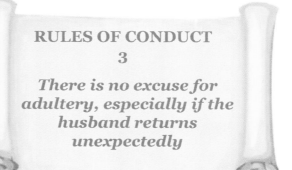

RULES OF CONDUCT
3

There is no excuse for adultery, especially if the husband returns unexpectedly

Perilous Passion

To be fair, it was not your fault. She wore gloves, which concealed her fingers. Invited to her residence in Kensington after the party it was too dark when she removed them to observe the presence of a wedding ring and anyway by that stage of the evening you had sunk too much champagne to care.

The clock on the local church was chiming two o'clock when you awoke from contented slumber alongside the young lady in question to hear a creaking noise. Dulled by the champagne, your brain did not raise the alarm until the bedroom door creaked again and a sliver of light emerged from the same direction. Quickly unravelling yourself from your sleeping partner you encountered the rings on her fingers, and blood froze in your veins.

Footsteps could now be heard advancing through the semi-darkness towards the bed. Trained by the army to slow your breathing in emergencies, you took a deep breath and assessed your options. The bedroom was on the second floor. Departure through the window would be hazardous without a ladder or rope, of uncertain availability. Attempts to dive under the bed would be equally futile given the proximity of the footsteps. The only practical option was to bolt for the door, grabbing your trousers and shoes on the way. Speed would be essential, particularly if he was carrying a gun or, heaven forbid, an axe.

The footsteps stopped at the bed. Fearfully you waited, poised for flight. A hand tugged the bedclothes.

'Mummy, I want to go to the bathroom,' said a little voice.

Gloves off

At last !

You have found her! Over there, in an attractive retro gown, poised and chic, stands the woman of your dreams. The tilt of her head, the confident manner she addresses the group of friends or acquaintances around her, the delightful way she laughs, everything about her represents the essence of feminine perfection. Heaven knows, you've seen enough women by now, studied them at close quarters, clothed and unclothed, to count yourself an expert in the matter, like a judge at a cattle show, a coarse comparison but accurate nonetheless.

You have met clever ones with intellectual accomplishments so far in advance of your own to diminish the prospect of a comfortable alliance, irascible ones with whom the intermittent bouts of physical rapture were scarcely worth hanging around for, moody ones who inhibited your natural gaiety and girls so tempestuous that you lived in fear of committing one of those indiscretions to which males are prone.

You have determined that, unlike dogs and horses, women do not respond satisfactorily to commands. Point at an old tennis ball lying in the grass and say 'fetch' to your retriever bitch and she will immediately lope off, collect the ball and place it at your feet, wagging her tail. Point at an empty whisky glass on the sideboard and say 'fill' to your girlfriend and you may end up in hospital. By trial and error you have determined that women share some of the attributes of the male with the added advantage that they can be encouraged to prepare dinner while you sit back admiring the attributes they do not share, viz shapely legs. Moreover, here is the crucial part, women are the only type of humans capable of helping out when the genetic trumpet blares in your ear proclaiming that the time is nigh for you to consider fatherhood.

So there she is, across a crowded room. You manoeuvre yourself through the throng to a position where you can hear her speak. Your knees tremble at the sweet music of her voice. Reversing into her as if by accident you join the group of friends or acquaintances where, apologizing profusely for your clumsiness, you steadily manipulate the thread of conversation to the point when you can modestly acknowledge a modicum of expertise in classical literature. You are careful not to exaggerate your academic qualifications, humbly admitting that you failed to accomplish the highest honours at Oxford. You are also careful not to monopolize the conversation. You take time dropping the hint that your commitment to the polo field was probably responsible for scuttling your chances of a double first.

She watches you through curled eyebrows, sizing you up. The other males in the group gradually disperse, outdone by your charismatic performance. She accepts your invitation for lunch. Over a bottle of Meursault at Claridges, she giggles attractively at your jokes. You escort her to the ballet at Convent Garden, to the opera at Glyndebourne, to Ascot where she wears a hat the size of the Albert Hall and signals her affection by taking your arm as you stroll to the paddock. On your part, you are bewitched by the lovely young woman and become increasingly possessive. When a handsome buck from a fashionable address in London attempts to muscle into your group at a Buckingham Palace garden party you jerk your knee into his groin explaining with mock regret as he limps away clutching his genitals that a skiing accident has affected the nerves in your leg rendering it liable to involuntary muscular spasms.

One starry night in Berkeley Square, to the sound of a nightingale singing, you drop onto aknee and present her with a ring, which she accepts.

31

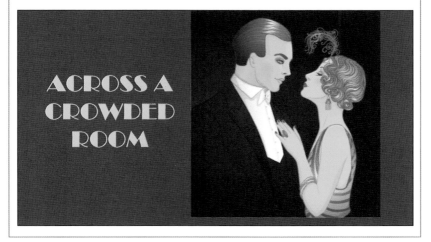

ACROSS A CROWDED ROOM

Mothers-in-Law

Be very careful . . .

You have selected your bride and are impatient to proceed. Naturally you have met her parents, established with relief that her mother is ageing well, comports herself elegantly, receives you with great affection and in the course of conversation displays exemplary wit and charm.

So that's alright then.

No, it is not ! What about the influence of your bride's mother on your lifestyle once the knot is tied and your patterns of behaviour become subject to scrutiny from this new and unaccustomed quarter? Mothers-in-law, even those agreeable on first acquaintance, are not renowned for the quality of mercy dispensed to unfortunate males who stray from the path of righteousness, particularly those with your track record.

It is prudent from the start to remain alert to the probability your movements will be subject to greater scrutiny than you would otherwise wish. Get into the habit of analyzing the potential consequences of, for example, disappearing to Paris for the weekend with 'Plunger' Perkins. The analysis of consequence - referred to as risk assessment (see opposite) - is commonly practised in industry. At the first sign of trouble, search the internet for 'risk assessment, mothers-in-law' and retain an appropriate expert.

A word of warning. Even if conditions eventually deteriorate to the extent that your mother-in-law can be heard at dinner expostulating loudly upon the list of suitors your wife misguidedly spurned, resist the temptation to search the internet for 'mothers-in-law, disposal of'. That would be going too far. Your wife, after all, may be fond of the old bat.

RULES OF CONDUCT
4
The impact of your wife's mother on your personal circumstances should be the subject of regular risk assessment

HSE	UK Health & Safety Executive		

(1) Affected party: ▨   (2) Assessment carried out by: ▨

Date of next review: ▨   Date assessment carried out: ▨

What are the hazards? (3)	Who might be harmed and how? (4)	What are you already doing to control the risks? (5)	What further action (6) do you need to take to control the risks?
▨	▨	▨	▨
▨	▨	▨	▨
▨	▨	▨	▨
▨	▨	▨	▨
▨	▨	▨	▨
▨	▨	▨	▨

Standard risk assessment template

Notes on use of risk assessment template

1. The affected party is normally yourself, although if you get caught in your mother-in-law's stables with a girl groom, the groom's prospects are not too hot either.

2. The initial assessment should be carried out by an expert (see text opposite).

3. Expert analysis will identify the hazards associated with visits to your mother-in-law's estate and vice-versa. Most of the hazards will arise from indiscretions on your part, viz inappropriate jokes at luncheon, being caught bathing with the vicar's daughter in the village pond etc.

4. The analysis should take into account prospective co-respondents of both sexes, viz chamber maids and junior governesses on one hand, proprietors of betting establishments and nightclub owners on the other. Prospective consequences of your indiscretions range from exhibitions of icy displeasure on the part of your mother-in-law to divorce by your wife. Servants are no longer flogged so, for them, enter 'dismissal' in the appropriate section of the column.

5. Self evidently the most appropriate precaution is to avoid being caught.

6. Mothers-in-law have been known to take alcohol. They are at their safest slumped in armchairs, eyes glazed. Keep her glass topped up.

Coitus Calamatosus

Honeymoon in Madeira

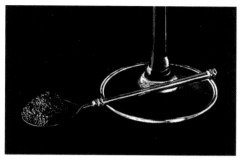

Caviar, for the right sort of people

The wedding is a glittering success attended by the right sort of people, properly dressed and conducting themselves gracefully, smiling at the photographers from society magazines with the right mixture of condescension and disdain, rationing themselves chivalrously to the caviar at the reception and making the right sort of noises during the speeches in the marquee. You depart proudly with your virgin bride in an open-top vehicle towing an assortment of objects including Fortnum and Mason cake tin lids and an enamel chamber pot.

She is quiet on the flight to Madeira, and quieter at dinner. You put it down to nervousness. You cheer her up with descriptions of the hotels you will be visiting on your way back through France. After dinner you change into your pyjamas and lope expectantly into the bedroom. To your dismay she is sitting on the side of the bed in a silk negligee, twisting a handkerchief in her hands, tears rolling down her face.

'I can't go through with this,' she sobs.

'Come now, it's not that bad,' you say comfortingly. 'Actually most people rather enjoy themselves, once they get going.'

'It's not that,' she sobs. 'You see, I'm in love with someone else.'

You are lost for words. 'Perhaps you should have cut corners and married him instead?' you blurt out eventually.

'It's not a him,' she said sobbing into her handkerchief.

Your jaw drops.

'That doesn't leave much in the way of options,' you point out, 'unless you've fallen for Terence, my parent's gay chauffeur?'

'I'm in love with my best friend, Arabella. Somehow I couldn't tell you. I'm so sorry. Please forgive me.'

Drunk as a Lord

Every bar from Monte Carlo to Paris . . .

You despatch your tearful bride home to seek an annulments and fly to Monte Carlo where the family chauffeur Terence is waiting, expecting to drive the newlywed couple back to England through France via luxury hotels, a gift from your parents. Instead you travel alone, sitting in the back of the limousine, bravely controlling your emotions and maintaining a stiff upper lip. By night you visit the local hostelries and pour your heart out to the pretty girls serving the customers, who don't understand what you are saying on account of your atrocious accent but smile sympathetically and murmur '*pauvre jeune homme*'.

Arriving in London you go straight to your club and drink yourself under a table. You are discovered next morning by a steward sweeping the floor.

'Shall I call a cab, sir?' enquires the steward helping you to your feet.

'Nobody loves me, Simkins,' you bleat.

'If you say so, sir,' says the steward.

'Do you love me, Simkins?'

'Of course, sir.'

'Deeply?'

'Very deeply, sir.'

'Thank you, Simkins, here's a fiver.'

'Much obliged, sir. I shall place the note in the staff box.'

'In exchange, I need some information.'

'I'll do my best, sir.'

'Where am I, Simkins?'

'In your club, sir.'

'I thought it looked familiar.'

The steward helps you into a taxi and quietly instructs the driver 'Take the poor young gentleman to his house in Berkeley Square.'

The table in question

Post Mortem

You worshipped her. You stood her on a pedestal. With hindsight, instead of respecting her virtue and treating her like an untouchable work of art, you should have made a pass at her, attempted a seduction that night in Berkeley Square instead of dropping on your knees and proposing matrimony. She would have resisted your advances and the tears would have flowed then, not later in Madeira, at the worst possible time. To the song of the nightingale she would have confessed that she was destined for the arms of women, not men, thereby saving you both a great deal of trouble.

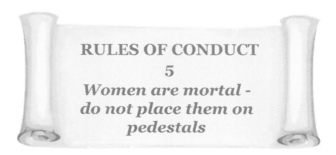

RULES OF CONDUCT
5
Women are mortal -
do not place them on
pedestals

Restoration

The annulment is granted. You return to your wisteria-clad cottage in Cirencester. You sleep badly, twisting and turning through the night, analysing what went wrong. Your friends do their best to cheer you up but at their parties you represent a doleful figure, lurking gloomily in dark corners, battling the pain of a broken heart.

Eventually 'Plunger' Perkins has had enough and takes you aside. 'Look here, this won't do. You're as much fun these days as a cold bath. Collect your books and we'll spend half term swotting for the finals in a little place I know.'

The little place is a tropical beach in Siam. 'Plunger' points at one of the luxurious bamboo cabins dotted amongst the palm trees. 'That's yours, and this is Lotus Leaf. She will look after you,' he says. You place the palms of your hands together in the Siamese fashion and bow at the golden-skinned girl with bright eyes and long dark hair. She returns your greeting. 'I will make you happy' she says, lowering her eyelashes.

To the sound of waves lapping the sand and the chattering of parrots in the palm fronds she makes you very happy indeed. She combs your hair in the mornings, sits at your feet while you work, tops up your glass with ice cubes and showers you when you return from bathing in the sea. She is happy too, she says, because the money she earns goes back to her village in the distant hills to finance a new road through the jungle. In gratitude the village elders are building her family a new hut and awarding her a handsome young man as husband.

Wistfully you return to Cirencester where a few weeks later, thanks to your studies, you pass your exams. 'Plunger' Perkins, who spent the entire vacation in bed with his maid, does not.

With bamboo cabins amidst the palm trees

Time to return home and take over the estate

Qualified to Succeed

You are now qualified by virtue of your academic and professional qualifications to succeed your father as master of the estate. You are sufficiently well read to receive guests with eloquence, and sufficiently informed of such matters as the pH content of soil and the marketing of cattle to administer the development of the land coming under your care. All you lack is a wife. Your parents are sympathetic. You dine together in the evenings in the great hall, your father at the head of the long table in the place you will inherit when your parents move to the smaller property being refurbished for them on the estate.

On your part, your emotions are still confused. Images of your virgin bride no longer disturb your sleep. Instead your mind keeps drifting back to the stretch of beach fringed by palm trees.

'Life was so uncomplicated. In different circumstances I could happily have settled down there,' you muse one day to your mother.

'Of course you couldn't, darling. There's more to a successful relationship than romantic interludes in bed. How would you generate income on a beach?' she enquires.

'Fishing.'

'What about wine?'

'Brew it.'

'And clothes?'

'You don't need any.'

'Don't be silly, darling. You can't go to church without trousers. Anyway, beaches are not your natural habitat. Men are heavily influenced by their background and the challenges of their social group. They benefit from choosing a partner equipped to meet those challenges, someone like Ophelia, for example.'

'Ophelia?'

'Yes, your childhood friend. You used to ride together, remember?'

Your heart skips a beat at the recollection of the mischievous eyes and your juvenile attempts at courtship.

'She's back from France. You'll meet her at dinner tomorrow.'

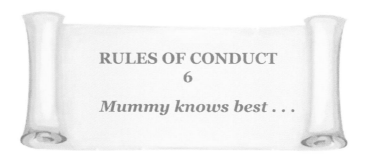

RULES OF CONDUCT
6

Mummy knows best . . .

The Envious Moon

Impatiently you wait next day for the sun to set over the ornamental lake. You hurry back from a meeting with the tenant farmers and change for dinner, bounding down the staircase adjusting the position of your black tie. You collect a cocktail from the tray and pretend to be engaged in a detailed examination of the ancestral painting above the fireplace when the guests arrive. You wait for the noise of greetings to subside before turning. You nearly drop your glass. Standing by the door with her parents is a gorgeous girl in a long silk gown, barely recognizable from the impish teenager with braces in her teeth who rode alongside with you at the pony club years ago. She takes your hand when you approach, leans forward and kisses your cheek. You stumble through some nonsensical reminiscences while she rolls her eyes playfully. She sits next to you at dinner. By the time the ladies withdraw from the table and the fragrance of their perfumes is replaced in the great hall by cigar smoke you are head over heels in love.

It is not just the oval shape of her face, or the way she wears her hair, or the spring in her step when she moves. She stares straight into your heart with those lovely lustrous eyes, releasing you from all shreds of pretence. You talk excessively in her presence, unburdening yourself, enraptured at the way she wrinkles her nose. She describes her time in Paris, in the art gallery where she worked, dodging the hands of the rich patrons, politely refusing to respond to their criticisms of England. The French are still morose about Agincourt, she says.

You meet every day. Evidently she finds you attractive and admits one afternoon when you are riding together that she had a great crush on you at school and used to wait for letters from you which never arrived. Dashing but unreliable, she says. She expands on the theme the moonlit night when you climb the ivy-clad walls to the balcony on the east wing to submit your proposal, a family tradition since the time of Shakespeare. Wise beyond her years she says 'I accept on the condition that, in the certainty you will stray, you will always come back to me'. Vehemently you deny the implication of the statement and vow to be a faithful husband, which is unlikely given the inherent fallibility of men, but you try hard and your love for Ophelia never fades. With increasing intensity her companionship becomes the most important feature of your life.

Acknowledgements

Every effort has been made to avoid copyright infringements, by tracing the sources of the artwork used in the text and, where applicable, by obtaining the appropriate permissions and licences.

In particular our thanks are extended to the executors of the Georges Barbier estate for the illustration adapted by our studio on page 4, the executors of the Charles Dana Gibson estate for the pen and ink portrait in page 20 and to Hatfield House for the photograph of the library used in page 37.

A Gentleman's Guide to Women
Part 1
A Gentleman's Guide to Women, Commoners & Cooking

Old English Press

Part 2

A Gentleman's Guide to Commoners

Introduction

The first thing to remember about commoners - customarily defined as persons brought up outside the direct influence of the court - is that there are lots of them. You will have already encountered members of the species in the role of servants and, with the notable exception of menopausal governesses, formed a favourable opinion of them.

Unfortunately the rules administering the conduct of servants does not apply to commoners living outside the boundaries of private estates and in the course of your travels you will encounter patterns of behaviour with which you will be unfamiliar, and which you may sometimes find disturbing. The purpose of this guide is to describe the manners and customs of commoners in order that you may understand the reasons for these patterns of behaviour, and thereby allow you to mix freely with ordinary people, without embarrassment, in a spirit of camaraderie.

It is a source of satisfaction that living standards for commoners have improved immeasurably over recent years. Gone are the days when workers shared their turf-roofed huts with pigs and sheep. It must be admitted that landowners have not always been assiduously committed to improving conditions for their employees. Looking back it is possible to sympathise with that unfortunate farm hand, seated on a stool on the muddy floor of his damp hovel smoking a clay pipe, who chose the occasion of a visit from his landowner, accompanied by a lady of distinction from a neighbouring estate, to complain of leaks in the turf roof. It must have been discomforting for the complainant to be informed by the ennobled lady 'My dear, don't change a thing, it's simply you!'

Nowadays the majority of commoners have exchanged their huts for stone houses and their donkey-carts and bicycles for motor cars. Indeed so rapid has been the pace of economic development that a number of commoners have been able to purchase estates for themselves and have begun the long journey by which their descendants may eventually receive invitations to the royal enclosure at Ascot.

You will already have met the sons of such families at school. They will help ensure that your time spent amidst ordinary people is trouble-free and enjoyable.

Contents

Transport, options

The most convenient method of transport is by motor car, with a chauffeur at the wheel and blinds drawn at the windows in urban areas to shut out the sight of ill-dressed people and garbage bins. The use of a chauffeur eliminates the problem of parking which is acute in city centres, particularly London. There the density of traffic represents a source of major inconvenience and sometimes forces gentlemen to walk to their destinations, in direct contact with commoners. Before considering the option read the section on 'Crowds'. The London underground railway system offers an alternative form of transport. However the system is not recommended for gentlemen on account of the pervasive smell of after shave lotion which admittedly keeps the carriages free of insects but can be distressing for persons of sensibility.

For long journeys to London, the best option is diesel, electric or, whenever possible, steam train. To avoid being disturbed during the journey by the noise of ordinary people or irritated by the supplementary odour of vinegar from potato crisp packages, gentlemen such as yourself sometimes prefer to take an entire carriage. Under this arrangement all the seats are marked RESERVED while you sit in the centre of the carriage in splendid isolation admiring the passing countryside, enjoying a light luncheon from a Fortnum & Mason's hamper.

Inevitably the arrangement provokes protests from the other carriages. 'Are all these seats taken?' is the normal enquiry, the first in a series of increasingly more strident ones ending with 'It's a diabolical liberty, that's what it is'. To keep commoners at bay it is prudent to travel with one of your gamekeepers. Armed with a 'Special Forces' badge he will explain to enquirers that you are a gentleman travelling under protective escort and that anyone attempting to enter the carriage will regrettably be shot. The added advantage of taking a gamekeeper is that, in the absence of porters at Paddington, he will carry your luggage to the taxi.

2

Crowds, traversing through

A curious fact about commoners is that they cannot walk in straight lines. Grouped together they meander along the road, weaving an uneven course, stopping intermittently to point out feature of the environment before resuming their passage, covering the entire extent of the roadway with their footsteps as they go. According to experts, the reason why commoners struggle to maintain a stable sense of direction is that they suffer from incomplete development of their powers of concentration, a medical condition known as *concentratus stuntus*.

Ordinarily you will be unaffected by the phenomenon, dismissing it as a matter of passing interest. Late for luncheon in London, however, struggling to make your way along Oxford Street towards your favourite oyster bar, impeded by crowds of shoppers ambling irregularly along the pavement, the matter takes on an entirely different hue.

The solution for accomplishing a trouble-free passage through crowds of commoners is to equip yourself with a bicycle bell. A few short bursts and the pedestrians in front of you will step hurriedly aside. In the unlikely event you experience adverse comment, nod sympathetically at the instigator and pass on. In extreme circumstances, if the crowd fails to part, you may need to use a foghorn. The blast from behind is sure to open a route for you. Unfortunately the concussive effect of a device designed to warn shipping twenty miles away is likely to result in casualties at close quarters. It may seem heartless to leave behind you a trail of bodies of elderly ladies, their shopping bags discharging tins of talcum powder onto the pavement as they topple forwards, but regrettably that is the price that commoners must pay for delaying a gentleman his oysters.

Social Contact
conversing with commoners

Now it's time to meet some ordinary people face to face. They will be nervous in your presence so start by putting them at ease. Smile broadly and break the ice by asking their names. For married couples, enquire about their children. This is guaranteed to loosen their tongues and you will soon be hearing how well Brenda and Kevin are doing at school. Be sure to compliment them on their children's scholastic progress before moving on.

Circulate extensively amongst the guests, chivalrously allowing yourself to be clutched on the arm by women whose attempts to deny the passage of time include dyeing their hair shades of fluorescent blue, who gushingly liken you to Cary Grant and introduce you to their friends who in turn shift uncomfortably on their feet as you proclaim your pleasure at making their acquaintance.

Commoners who have risen through the ranks to reach important positions - directors of national companies and high court judges for example - possess a much firmer grasp of the principles of social engagement and with them you can raise your game a little, even to the extent of introducing humour into your discourse although you should avoid the one about the actress and the bishop when talking to senior clerics. With luck you will find a few individuals amongst the upper echelons of successful commoners capable of developing themes of general interest. Whether the subject of discussion is interesting or not, however, the trick is to maintain an attitude of delighted wonder at the erudition of the people you meet, hanging on bravely through subjects such as the weather, cultivation of Brussels sprouts and infallible methods of escaping from the bunkers at Sunningdale until, released from your ordeal, you can meet up with 'Basher' Bingham and make for your club.

Clothes, frightfulness of

Commoners are notoriously incapable of dressing themselves with any semblance of style. Nothing is more depressing than to witness groups of ordinary people meandering through the streets, the males in gym shoes (optimistically referred to as trainers), jeans (a form of garment favoured by cattle hands in America) and tee shirts (often decorated with the faces of popular jungle music performers), the females in costumes mistakenly labelled by their fashion magazines as *chic*, mostly manufactured in Pakistan.

The simplest way of tidying up the streets and restoring the aesthetic grandeur of England's civic environment would be to follow the example of fifteenth century Florence and introduce regulations on the types of clothing worn in public. Commoners would be issued with smocks, a functional multi-purpose garment manufactured locally. White or cream coloured versions would be supplied to office and indoor workers, grey smocks to outside labourers and traditional brown smocks to factory and farm workers. Thus dressed in neutral colours, ordinary people would blend into the background instead of despoiling the country's architectural heritage with the outlandish hues of their contemporary apparel.

Commoners would be amongst the first to see the advantages of the proposal, the cost savings in household budgets, the absence of 'what shall I wear today' cries from their wives and daughters, the economic benefit to the country as a whole from increased number of tourists to Britain and the improved foreign exchange differential with Pakistan.

Amongst those exempt from the requirement to wear smocks would be university graduates, thereby ensuring an upsurge in academic activity within the lower orders of society. Commoners wanting to litter foreign palm-fringed beaches with beer cans would have to start studying too, the privilege of owning a passport being confined to the gentry and possessors of college degrees.

5

Self Importance

attitudes of

Commoners are inclined to adopt unbecoming airs and graces when deployed in positions of authority. A gentleman should maintain composure in such circumstances. The following examples illustrate the extent of the problem.

Example 1

PHARMACIST'S ASSISTANT (fussily reading the label as she brings your prescription to the counter): Have you taken these pills before?

GENTLEMAN: Yes, for several years.

PHARMACIST'S ASSISTANT: Are you aware of the side effects?

GENTLEMAN: Thank you, yes.

PHARMACIST'S ASSISTANT: Are you aware that side effects include palpitations, giddiness, nausea and constipation?

GENTLEMAN: As I said, I've taken them before.

PHARMACIST'S ASSISTANT: And that external side effects include piles, warts and nits?

GENTLEMAN: Yes, if you could just pass me the . . .

PHARMACIST'S ASSISTANT (drawing herself up magisterially): There's no need to adopt that attitude with me, sir.

GENTLEMAN: I can assure you . . .

PHARMACIST'S ASSISTANT (delivering the package dismissively across the counter): Next please.

Example 2

SHOP ASSISTANT: Are you paying by cash or card?

GENTLEMAN: Card.

SHOP ASSISTANT: Kindly place it in the machine for me.

GENTLEMAN: For you, or for me?

SHOP ASSISTANT (blankly): Pardon?

GENTLEMAN: Is this transaction for your benefit, or mine?

SHOP ASSISTANT (rolling eyes and looking over shoulder): Mr Jenkins, can you spare a minute?

SHOP MANAGER: Yes, sir, what seems to be the trouble?

GENTLEMAN: If your assistant's request was confined to "kindly place the card in the machine" omitting the "for me", it would minimise the impression of superiority.

SHOP MANAGER: I'm so sorry, sir. Please accept my apologies for any inconvenience.

GENTLEMAN: Not at all.

SHOP MANAGER: Do you wish to continue with the purchase?

GENTLEMAN: By all means.

SHOP MANAGER: Are you paying by cash or card, sir?

GENTLEMAN: Card.

SHOP MANAGER: Excellent, sir, kindly place it in the machine for me.

The Law
avoiding brushes with

Not so long ago the legal profession turned a blind eye to the indiscretions of the gentry. Policemen tolerated the eccentricities of the upper classes, ensuring that persons of good birth were not unduly inconvenienced by the comings and goings of ordinary people. Two examples from the period will suffice.

Example 1

POLICEMAN (patrolling beat in Mayfair): Good evening, sir.

GENTLEMAN (dressed in top hat, white tie and tails, clutching lamppost, after a night of champagne and brandy): Just the chap.

POLICEMAN (stopping): Can I be of assistance, sir?

GENTLEMAN: You certainly may, constable. Be a good fellow and tell me if my thing is hanging out.

POLICEMAN (looking down): No sign of it, sir.

GENTLEMAN: Dammit, I'm wetting my trousers again.

Example 2

POLICEMAN: Where were you at the time of the accident, sir?

GENTLEMAN : In my Bentley, and it wasn't an accident, it was deliberate.

POLICEMAN (later, in court, reading to the magistrate from his notebook): The accused admitted to driving his vehicle backwards and forwards, ramming the cars behind and in front of him, causing extensive damage to those vehicles in the process, your honour.

MAGISTRATE (to gentleman in dock): Good morning, Henry. How's your father?

GENTLEMAN: Excellent, thank you. He won at Chepstow last week.

MAGISTRATE: Well done him. Give him my regards, Now then, what's this about damaged cars?

GENTLEMAN: I was simply trying to get out of my parking space. The blighters had hemmed me in.

MAGISTRATE: Upon my soul.

GENTLEMAN: So I adjusted their positions with the Bentley, and drove off.

MAGISTRATE: Quite right. How inconsiderate of them. Constable, tell the plaintiffs to park properly next time. Case dismissed.

Things have changed since then. The police force has modernised, to the detriment of a gentleman's high spirits. So don't throw your weight about or expose yourself on the pavement at midnight. Above all, don't try to buy yourself out of trouble with a twenty pound donation to the annual policemen's ball stuffed into a constable's pocket. You might find yourself sharing a prison cell with persons who regularly split infinitives. An unenviable prospect.

Table Manners
development of

Commoners have taken enormous strides in improving the mechanics of eating. Fingers are no longer employed to grab portions of food from the table and gravy is no longer slurped from uplifted plates. Nowadays the use of hands is mostly confined to those immigrant communities which in accordance with long and noble traditions employ bread or lumps of rice as the means of transferring food to their mouths.

The native population has adapted to the use of cutlery well, and great progress has been made in the proper handling of knives and forks. Indeed amongst the upper echelons of commoner society, at the high tables of universities for example, the art of dining elegantly has been mastered to a significant degree of competence.

So you should not be unduly discomforted when joining ordinary people for luncheon or dinner. A few simple tips. Watch your host and hostess carefully. Follow their example. If they eat with their elbows on the table and decline second helpings with the words 'Thank you but I am fully replete' then you should do the same. Given the pace of social development these days you should almost certainly be spared the indignity of having to join a chorus of 'Cheers' or 'Bottoms up' when raising your wine glass to your lips.

$\mathcal{M}obs,$ *dealing with*

It is early evening in London. You are taking exercise before dinner and have walked further than usual, lost in thought, planning in your mind the guest list for a weekend in Biarritz, in particular whether to include 'Hairy' Hargreaves in the party in view of his conduct during the last outing involving the wife of the Austrian consul with whom he was discovered under a beach umbrella at dawn, when you realise you have strayed into unfamiliar territory. The streets are narrow and the shops are boarded up. You pause, wondering whether to continue or retrace your steps. Uneasy at the hostile environment, you turn to find your way blocked by four unpleasant-looking individuals, one of whom is brandishing a knife. What do you do?

OPTION 1
Throw your wallet onto the pavement and run like smoke.

OPTION 2
Tell the unpleasant-looking individuals to gather round and address them on the following lines. 'Now look here, lads. If you're hoping for cash, I never carry the stuff. Moreover I should warn you that I played rugby football at school. It's important to speak frankly on the subject because you seem like nice chaps and I don't want you getting hurt. So disperse quietly, and I'll say no more about it.' Then set off briskly back to your club.

Note:
The editor would be interested to hear from readers who selected the second option in similar circumstances and survived their injuries.   11

$\mathcal{D}ogs$, *controlling numbers of*

Travelling from your estate it will quickly become apparent that the reason sea levels are rising in Britain is less to do with climate change than that the weight of excrement deposited on the pavements by dogs is causing the islands to sink. It becomes equally apparent that the majority of commoners fail to look after their dogs properly, and that most of the unfortunate animals rely on household television programmes for the sight of grass or the open fields for which they yearn and on which they were originally bred.

You will find that members of your club in London unanimously support the introduction of licenses for ownership of non-working dogs. You join them to fulminate at the spineless government officials who tremble in the face of liberal protest groups which would rather our islands sank than deprive commoners of their rights to make dogs miserable.

You design an application form for a domestic dog licence (see opposite) and send it to *The Times* for publication. The document is declined with a note of regret from the newspaper. Determined to promote the cause you argue in its favour at cocktail parties where eventually you are challenged by a young lady who stares at you angrily.

'How dare you presume to regulate the lives of ordinary decent people! Does it occur to you that some people might be as lonely as the poor animals they rescue from dog pounds? You should be ashamed of yourselves, descending from your grouse moor to lecture hard working citizens on their manners and behaviour. The sooner the world is rid of idle rich dilettantes like yourself the better!' she says, her attractive bosom heaving with emotion.

This stops you in your tracks. Thoughtfully you peer into the warm recesses of her blouse.

'I say,' you say, 'are you available for dinner this evening?'

by appointment to
Oodles Dining Club, Mayfair

SOCIETY FOR PROTECTION OF DOGS FROM THEIR OWNERS

LICENCE APPLICATION FORM

1   Are you a little old lady ?   [yes] [no]

If yes, proceed with purchase of lap dog, no licence required

2   Are you a male with shaven head and tattoos ?   [yes] [no]

If yes, permission for dog licence is refused. Report immediately to nearest police station where you are probably wanted for something

3   Are you a moderately sensible person ?   [yes] [no]

If yes, proceed to next question

4   Are you aware that the average family-size dog requires one hour's exercise each day off the leash in open countryside ?   [yes] [no]

If yes, proceed to next question

5   What do you propose to do about it ?

5.1 Change your job to allow two hour's transport each day in search of open countryside, and one hour for dog exercise

5.2 Allocate responsibility for looking after the dog to your wife

5.3 Buy a gerbil

You will be notified of our decision by post

Acknowledgements

Every effort has been made to avoid copyright infringements, by tracing the sources of the artwork used in the text and, where applicable, by obtaining the appropriate permissions and licences.

A Gentleman's Guide to Commoners
Part 2
A Gentleman's Guide to Women, Commoners & Cooking

Old English Press

Part 3

A Gentleman's Guide to Cooking

Preface

These recipes are intended for gentlemen forced under circumstances beyond their control, or the result of one or more indiscretions, to fend for themselves in the kitchen. Herein will be found dishes comfortably familiar to gentlemen young and old from spells at boarding school, university, club, military establishment or embassy. The recipes are simple to execute and sufficiently varied to give pleasure should the sequence need to be repeated during an extended absence of wife and kitchen staff. So varied and pleasurable indeed that on return to normality he may find himself foregoing his accustomed position on his shooting stick at his favourite copse, gun ready, retriever poised at his feet, in order to savour, for example, more of the cheese straws featured on page 8.

Several of the recipes herein involve the use of an oven. Statistics indicate that men are more likely than women to drop a roasting pan, thereby ruining luncheon and spattering their trousers with hot oil and pieces of onion. Appropriate cautions and warnings are included in the text. The recipes are sized for one to two people. With the exception of fresh asparagus, vegetables are largely ignored. Gentlemen do not care for them much, rightly so, having endured those endless mounds of tasteless green beans at school, extruding enough string to suspend Faversham minor from the rafters by his feet. When referenced herein it is assumed that the vegetables in question have been treated with sufficient salt, pepper, butter and, as appropriate, cream to render them edible. The recipes exclude the use of garlic, an ingredient much favoured by foreigners and commoners but not gentlemen, especially those with duties at court.

Contents

Introduction

If upon awakening you find yourself in a condition of discomfort, arising perhaps from excessive consumption of wine at someone's manor last night and the unfortunate attempt to impress a young lady by swinging through the dining room window, closed at the time. You would prefer to remain in bed and nurse your discomfort but work awaits, not least the drawing of a cheque to cover the cost of manor house dining room repairs. You will feel better after a hot shower and breakfast. Unfortunately the kitchen staff are off duty and your wife is in Milan filing for divorce. The answer of course is a boiled egg, the simplest possible breakfast, trouble free, delicious and completely safe provided someone in your condition does not burn himself on the stove, scald himself with boiling water or slice himself with the knife.

For the sake of aesthetic presentation the egg in the illustration below has been decorated with greenery. Unless you are a competent horticulturist, conversant with herbs, avoid this step. Stumble back from the garden across the dew-soaked lawn in your dressing gown and slippers clutching a handful of hemlock and your recovery will be compromised.

𝕹otes

Boiled Egg

Note:
A simplified version of this diagram is available from the editor on request

Ingredients
Fresh egg
Salt
Pepper

Accompaniments
Bread (toasted as required)
Butter
Marmalade
Coffee

Cooking
Collect egg from hen, place on spoon (egg not hen) and lower into pan of boiling water. After three to four minutes, retrieve egg from pan (using spoon), remove head (of egg) with knife, season contents with salt and pepper and consume.

3

Introduction

There are innumerable reasons for the prolonged absence of a wife.
Shopping, for example. Tempted deep into Harrods, she lost track of time,
spent the night with a friend who knew a little stall in Shepherd Market
specializing in antique porcelain doorknobs next to a little restaurant where
they met some more friends etc. Visiting her ancestral home is another, a
convenient location at which to discuss your manifold shortcomings with a
sympathetic audience, particularly your irritating habit of using her
bathroom window to blast pigeons from the walls of the vegetable garden
with your shotgun, the memory of which sends her weeping to her mother's
lap wailing regret at not having married into the Household Cavalry. There
could be more subtle reasons for her absence, including failure to observe
the fourth anniversary of the demise of her spaniel Simone de Beauvoir,
tragically set upon by hounds of the Heythrop Hunt, but the most perilous
involve members of the feminine sex. Whereas it is acceptable for a wife
to flutter her eyes demurely or otherwise at her guests, the first sign of such
behaviour on the part of the husband represents grounds for divorce.

So, alas, the pretty young oriental kitchen maid you greeted a few moments
ago on the doorstep in your dressing gown must be sent back to her agency
before your wife returns on the London express laden with Harrods
shopping bags. Seize your phrase book and find something on the lines of
'Sorry about this but, before you go, would you mind preparing that prince
of English breakfasts, bubble and squeak with crispy bacon?' If the girl
declines, prepare the dish yourself, proceeding in accordance with the
recipe opposite

Bubble & Squeak

"When you've finished, climb out through the pantry window, here's a tenner for the bus"

Ingredients

500g mashed potato, whipped with butter and cream
250g boiled and shredded cabbage
Slices of bacon
Butter, salt and pepper

Accompaniments

Coffee

Cooking

Combine the mashed potato with shreds of cooked cabbage, season with salt and pepper and knead into pancake size pieces. Fry the pieces at medium heat in butter, duly observing the bubbling & squeaking protests of the cabbage, until the pancakes are hot and golden brown. Grill the bacon. Serve with the bubble & squeak, and coffee. sighing with pleasure at this most satisfactory combination of ingredients.

Introduction

The commonplace breakfast – bacon, egg, sausage, tomato etc - is largely devoid of taste nowadays, relying more on quantity than quality. Good bacon is hard to find, sausages are stuffed with bread, and tomatoes are inclined to explode their contents down the front of your shirt when pierced with a knife. In particular we mourn the passing of the English sausage, once deserving a salver of its own on the sideboard now, with rare exceptions, fit only for unwelcome guests and dogs. If you are fortunate enough to live within range of a butcher who purveys sausages properly filled with seasoned pork or beef then the variety of your breakfasts may be correspondingly increased. Sausages are easy to cook and preparation requires no instruction. Even better, treat yourself to that most celebrated of ancestral dishes, devilled kidneys. In terms of taste, the commonplace breakfast served in most contemporary establishments pales by comparison.

*Succulent lamb's kidneys in a rich
brown sauce*

Notes

Devilled Kidneys

Dick Turpin invariably breakfasted on devilled kidneys before going to work

Ingredients

4 lambs' kidneys
2 tbsp flour
30g soft butter
1/2 tsp cayenne pepper
1/2 tsp mustard powder

1 tsp Worcestershire sauce
1 tsp anchovy sauce or puree
thick slice bread
slices of bacon
olive oil, salt, pepper

Accompaniment
Coffee

Cooking

Trim the kidneys, slice in half laterally so they retain their shape, and remove the white fatty cores. Dust the kidneys in the flour seasoned with cayenne pepper, salt and mustard powder. Fry each side for two minutes in the butter, with Worcestershire and anchovy sauces added. In a separate pan, fry the bacon and bread in olive oil until the bacon is crispy and bread is golden brown. Combine on a breakfast plate, with the kidneys and juices on the fried bread.

'And more cheese straws, please'

Notes

Caution
You are allowed to use the oven for this recipe
on the basis you couldn't possibly burn down
the house preparing such a simple dish

Cheese Straws

Introduction

Cheese straws have been popular in Britain for centuries. The inscription *'amo caseus culmi'* discovered at an archaeological site in Canterbury recently indicates that the Romans liked them too, and were probably responsible for their introduction to these islands. Delicious on their own or with champagne as the sun bursts through the leaves on the trees lining the paddock, cheese straws are the perfect refreshment to punctuate the gap between breakfast and luncheon. However be careful while transporting them as they are likely to crumble in your pocket if, for example, you happen to embrace a young lady on your way to the stables.

Ingredients

1 1/2 cups grated mixed hard cheese such as Parmesan, Red Leicester and aged Cheddar
375g packet puff pastry
Milk, for brushing
Flour, for preparation
1/4 tsp cayenne pepper

Accompaniment

Champagne

fresh from the oven

Cooking

Preheat oven to 200°C (180°C fan). Cut the block of puff pastry lengthways into 6 to 8 equal strips. On a floured surface roll out each strip lengthways until it's about 3-5ml thick. Spoon the cheese on to one half of each of the pastry strips and sprinkle cheese with cayenne pepper. Fold the plain half of each pastry strip over the cheese-covered half. Hold each end of the pastry strip in your hands and twist a couple of times. Brush with a little milk. Place on a baking tray and bake in the oven until golden brown, about 20 to 25 minutes

9

Introduction

This princely soup, served hot or cold, accompanied by bread and wine, is sufficient in the way of luncheon for a gentleman unexercised in the morning. There are several claimants for the honour of the soup's invention. Louis XV of France is one. By the time his tasters had demonstrated that the exquisite mixture was free of poison, the soup was cold, hence its reputation as a summer dish. Louis Diat, chef at the Ritz-Carlton in New York, who grew up in Montmarault in the Allier department near the spa resort town of Vichy, is another. He claimed the honour in 1917 on behalf of America, which has vociferously championed the assertion ever since. In reality the sublimely successful effect of mixing potatoes, leeks and cream with chicken stock was discovered in a Welsh valley in 1872 by Gruffydd and Clywd Jenkins, a farmer and his wife whose married life was spent contentedly rearing sheep and trying to pronounce each other's names. Returning from the fields one evening Gruffydd accidentally knocked over a cream jug into a combination of vegetable and chicken stock, and the legend was born. The fame of the Jenkins' soup eventually reached New York where Chef Louis Diat copied the recipe, renamed it 'Vichyssoise' and claimed it for his own.

This princely soup . . .

𝔑otes

Vichyssoise

*Gruffydd and Clywd Jenkins,
inventors of Vichyssoise soup*

Ingredients

2 cups finely diced raw potatoes
125g butter
6 leeks, cleaned and cut into pieces
1 chicken cube
3 cups water

2 cups sour cream or heavy cream
1/4 tsp nutmeg
Salt/pepper
Chopped chives

Accompaniment

French bread

Cooking

Boil potatoes in salted water, drain and reserve. Melt butter in pan and cook the leeks gently for a few minutes. Add the chicken cube and 3 cups water and bring to boil. Lower the heat and simmer the leeks until tender. Add the potatoes, season to taste with salt, pepper and nutmeg. Put mixture in blender and process for 1 minute, or until smooth. When ready to serve, pour in cream and decorate with chives. Remember to fix lid firmly to blender before pressing button or you will need a change of clothes.

Introduction

There are two ways to prepare this splendid soup. The first is to purchase a live lobster, cook it with as much inconvenience as possible to the majestic crustacean, reserve the meat, and boil the shell as the basis for the broth. The second is to purchase a can of lobster soup from an appropriate establishment and embellish the contents appropriately. Recipes for both options are provided on the opposite page.

The tricky part of the first recipe is the catching and slaying of the lobster which would put up a good fight if the fishermen who fetched it from the deep hadn't reduced its chances of defence by securing its claws with sturdy rubber bands. That is the first thing to check when collecting a live lobster from the larder where it has spent the night angrily reviewing its options, because if the rubber bands have split and its claws are waving menacingly in the air you should probably abandon the project and let someone competent take over, like your cook or wife on their return to the house, or your six year old daughter after school.

red if dead

Assuming the lobster is still alive and shackled, transport it to the kitchen table and plan the execution. In the old days that would involve dropping the blue-black crustacean into a pan of boiling water and waiting until it turned red, ignoring the muffled screams which you were told represented the noise of air bubbles expanding in its shell. Nowadays the humane way of slaying a lobster is to drive a sharp object through its head above the eyes. So fetch a sturdy knife and proceed with the task. Go on, get on with it . . . On second thoughts, time is running out and the lawn needs mowing for croquet . The second recipe looks more convenient.

Lobster Bisque

Recipe 1

Ingredients

8 cups water
2 cups dry white wine
1 chicken stock cube
1 live lobster
1/2 cup butter
1 cup onion finely diced
1 vegetable stock cube

1/2 cup self-raising flour
1 1/2 cups canned tomatoes
1 tsp paprika
1/2 tsp thyme
1/4 tsp ground red pepper
1/4 cup brandy
1 cup heavy cream

Cooking

Place the water and white wine into a large pot and boil. Place lobster (deceased) and chicken stock cube in the broth. Reduce heat to medium and cook covered for approximately 6 minutes. Turn lobster with tongs and cook covered for another 6 minutes. Remove lobster from broth. When cool, remove white meat, chop into small pieces and reserve. Strain the broth through a sieve into a container and reserve.

Discard lobster shell. Combine butter and flour into empty pot and heat until mixture begins to darken. Add tomatoes, brandy and vegetable stock cube dissolved in cup (additional) of hot water. Add the paprika, thyme and ground pepper and the reserved lobster broth. Cook uncovered for 30 minutes under medium low heat, stirring frequently so not to burn. Add chopped lobster meat and heavy cream, and serve.

Recipe 2

Preparations

Purchase can of lobster soup

Cooking

Heat contents in pan, add dash of cognac and dollop of cream, serve.

Introduction

Supposedly conceived in the kitchens of Windsor Castle from the remnants of dinner the previous night and adopted enthusiastically by the parsimonious Victorians this watery gruel became an indispensable part of a gentleman's diet, feasted upon throughout the empire in regimental tents, government houses, cavalry clubs, from the residences of district officers in mountainous regions of Africa to the grandest clubs in imperial India where men of impeccably loyal disposition would dab their moustaches dry and proclaim 'By Jove, that was jolly fine' on the basis that if the unpalatable broth was good enough for the monarch in Windsor it was good enough for them. Liberal applications of sherry pepper into the bowl went some way to masking the disagreeable taste.

The recipe herein is repeated in its original form from Victorian cookbooks, designed to take you back to those good old days at preparatory school or college when, hungry and hopeful, you were at the mercy of barely competent cooks. As a precaution, drop a hot chilli into a bottle of cooking sherry the night before.

Deceptively awful . . .

𝕹otes

𝔅𝔯𝔬𝔴𝔫 𝔚𝔦𝔫𝔡𝔰𝔬𝔯 𝔖𝔬𝔲𝔭

Responsible for the unappetizing dish which bears its name ?

Ingredients

Mangled remnants of roast meat/game
Onion
Salt
Pepper

Accompaniments

Sherry pepper

Cooking

Boil the remnants of meat/game in water for fifteen minutes. Add the onion, finely sliced. Boil for further fifteen minutes. Remove scum from top of pan. Serve hot.

Introduction

Naturally you are familiar with the great French sauces. You have travelled extensively and dined in the finest restaurants, from the George Cinq in Paris to Lord Jim's on the second floor of the Oriental Hotel in Bangkok. You can tell the difference between Hollandaise, Velouté, Béchamel and Béarnaise and describe their principal features without hesitation. Do you know how to prepare them? Of course not. Production of the great sauces is a job for experts excelling in culinary techniques and frankly the only thing you excel at, apart from shooting pheasants, is reciting 'Mary had a Little Lamb' backwards in Latin. Never mind. Substitutes for the great French sauces are easily prepared. On the opposite page you will find details of simple alternatives that should see you through your period of atonement.

The gardens of the Oriental Hotel in which you smoked a cheroot

𝔑otes

𝕾𝖆𝖚𝖈𝖊𝖘

Mustard Cream Sauce

A delicious multi-purpose sauce for shellfish, meat and game in which finely chopped shallots, sautéed in butter, are combined with brandy, mustard, cream and herbs. Refer to page 33 to see the recipe in action.

Port Gravy

Into a roasting pan from which the roasted fowl, meat or game has been removed for carving, sprinkle flour over the cooking juices. Apply heat to the pan, and add 50g butter and a glass of port. Stir mixture thoroughly, adding small amounts of boiling water as required to achieve the right consistency, and you will end up with a delicious thick gravy. Refer to page 31 to see the recipe in action.

Carruther's Gold

Almost indistinguishable in taste and texture from the fabled Hollandaise sauce this simple blend was stumbled upon by a district officer in the Pacific region of the British empire circa 1910 to accompany baby bamboo shoots, the local equivalent of asparagus.

125g salted butter
1 cup milk
2 tsp cornflour
2 egg yolks

Carruther's Gold

Stir cornflour into milk. Melt 125g butter in saucepan, add the milk and stir until the mixture thickens. Add a little more cornflour as necessary to achieve required thickness. When thickening is finished, add egg yolks and stir gently into the sauce as it turns golden.

Note: Substitute arrowroot powder for the cornflour, in slightly greater quantities, to accomplish a sheen that Hollandaise sauce would be proud of.

A shrimping expert of times past

Notes

Potted Shrimps

Catch, Prepare and Dine

Catch

To capture the subject of this unparalleled delicacy, dress yourself in waders and cricket blazer and proceed to the seaside with a shrimping net (for design, see opposite). You need a coastline with an extensive flat beach where the tide runs out a long way. Time your arrival to coincide with the ebb, and enter water. The purpose of the waders is to keep your trousers dry. The blazer will mark you down as a person of distinction and avoid you being confused with ordinary shrimpers. Keep an eye on the water level. The tide can return swiftly and nothing looks more ridiculous than someone in a cricket jacket flailing around in the sea, out of his depth, shouting for help.

Prepare

With aptitude you will have captured sufficient of the treasured brown shrimps (*Crangon crangon*) to constitute the major part of luncheon or the first course for dinner. Boil the catch for two minutes in salted water. Drain, peel and insert into ramekins. Melt sufficient butter, spiced with cayenne pepper and grated nutmeg to taste. Compact the mixture while filling the ramekins to the top with the butter. Refrigerate briefly before serving, to harden the top.

Dine

Eat with ciabatta bread for lunch, or with toast for dinner.

Purchase and Dine

Purchase tubs of potted shrimps from an appropriate merchant, warm briefly in oven or microwave before serving so that surface of butter is just on the point of melting. Eat with ciabatta bread for lunch, or with toast as a starter for dinner.

Introduction

The rule is perfectly clear. A gentleman maintains a side of Scottish smoked salmon in his larder whenever the seasons allow. He does not purchase the packaged variety, except in emergencies. Whenever possible he maintains rights to the River Spey and catches the fish himself. He cures and smokes the catch on his estate, except when resident in London where civic bylaws prohibit the seasonal erection of smokeries in, for example, St James's Park forcing him into arrangements with appropriate merchants at Billingsgate market. A gentleman is aware of the difference between the coarse red texture of foreign salmon and the creamy pink exquisiteness of their Scottish counterparts.

First, catch your salmon

𝕹otes

𝔖moked 𝔖almon

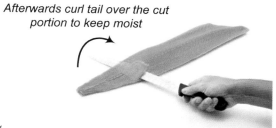

Afterwards curl tail over the cut portion to keep moist

Slicing

Select a long sharp supple knife with plenty of width. Check that all bones have been removed from the fish (they are easily visible, and easily plucked out with pliers). Ensure the salmon will not slip on its board, it needs to remain steady as you carve.

Start at the tail, working back towards it. The first few slices will be narrower and drier than the rest (reserve these for your mother-in-law). Continue slicing back towards the tail, gradually moving up the fish. You should be able to see the blade of the knife through the salmon (which is how you know the slices are thin enough).

Each time the blade of the knife reaches the skin, change the angle and continue along the surface of the skin to collect all the salmon. The skin is tough and will not part unless you deliberately slice vertically down. When only a few slices are required, flip the tail back over to cover the unsliced portion and keep the area moist.

Serving

Serve only with buttered brown bread and a slice of lemon. There is no need for further embellishment, other than chilled dry white wine. The texture of a great Scottish smoked salmon is creamier than the crème fraiche accompaniment sometimes circulated by hostesses anxious to mask the inferior quality of a hurried purchase.

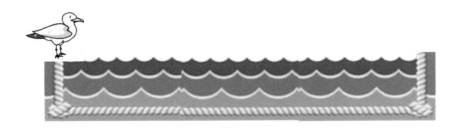

Introduction

Ranked by many as the finest fish in the world, the sweet and buttery Dover sole commands a hefty price at Billingsgate market and is not always conveniently available to estates north of the Thames. Should you be idling your way through the pantry in the absence of your wife and kitchen staff looking for sustenance and observe the distinctive shape of a Dover sole lurking on a shelf or in the refrigerator, smile lavishly and set about the task, unfamiliar to many but simple in principle, of removing the rough brown skin from its front and white skin from its back. Incise the skin at the tail, grasp the skin and pull sharply which, with sufficient strength, will peel from the fish with the noise of a plaster being ripped from your leg. After skinning the fish on both sides, cut off its head and fins using sturdy kitchen scissors. Clean the blood from the spine, wash the fish and pat dry with towel. You are now only a few minutes away from enjoying one of the globe's truly magnificent dishes.

Incise with
sharp knife

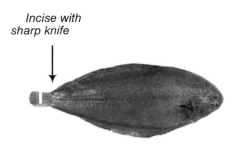

𝔑otes

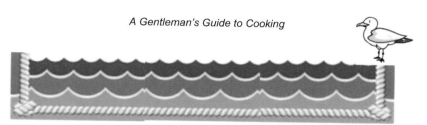

𝕯𝖔𝖛𝖊𝖗 𝕾𝖔𝖑𝖊

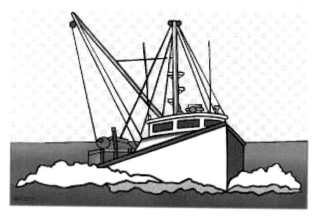

Ingredients

Dover sole
Olive oil
Butter
Lemon

Accompaniments

Carruther's gold sauce (see page 17)
Expensive dry white wine

Cooking

Brush fish lightly with olive oil and melted butter and grill for 2 minutes either side, adjusting temperature if flames arise. Alternatively fry the fish for slightly longer at medium heat in olive oil and butter, turning once and basting frequently. Do not insult a Dover sole with vegetables or potatoes. Serve the great fish with Carruther's gold sauce, a great wine (eg Mersault), a slice lemon and, if you must, a salad.

Introduction

Yes, we know, it was disgusting, served with watery boiled potatoes and peas as hard as shotgun pellets. Never mind, you are grown up now, the master of your own destiny. Since your schooldays, ways have been found of cooking mince the results of which are not only edible but sufficiently agreeable to warrant second helpings. So stranded again in your rural pile without wife, cook or servant in sight roll up your sleeves, top up your glass, and set about the recipe opposite.

'It's not mince again today, do you suppose?'

Notes

Cottage Pie

Ingredients

2 tbsp olive oil
500g beef mince
1 onions, finely chopped
2 small carrots, chopped
2 celery sticks, chopped
2 tbsp plain flour

1 tbsp tomato purée
large glass red wine
450 ml beef stock
2 tbsp Worcestershire
few thyme sprigs
2 tsp paprika
25g butter

For potatoes:
2 large potatoes, chopped
100 ml milk
25g butter
50g strong cheddar, grated
freshly grated nutmeg
salt, pepper

Cooking

Brown the mince and onions together in large pan. Mix flour into wine, add tomato purée, stir until flour dissolved. Add mixture to pan of simmering mince. Add beef cube to 450 ml water, and stir into pan. Add chopped carrots, chopped celery, Worcestershire sauce, butter and paprika. Simmer for 45 minutes or longer, until mixture thickens into thick dark gravy, seasoning with add and pepper as required.

Separately boil and mash the potatoes, adding milk, butter, cheese, nutmeg and salt and pepper to taste. Ladle mince into casserole dish and cover with mashed potatoes. If likely to be joined for luncheon by attractive female, create artistic design on top of mashed potatoes using fork. Place casserole dish in hot oven (220oC) for 30 minutes or until surface is golden brown.

There you are, in the distance, with that girl you will never forget . . .

𝔑otes

A Gentleman's Guide to Cooking

𝕾𝖙𝖊𝖆𝖐 𝕱𝖗𝖎𝖙𝖊𝖘

Introduction

The years have passed but you still remember that visit to Paris at the café where chic and impatient she plucked the menu, which you had been struggling to translate, from your hands and ordered steak frites for two. Later in the week at her apartment overlooking the Seine she had demonstrated how to prepare the dish, adding water to control the temperature of the steak (water, for heaven's sake!) and the result was stupendous. The French are born with these skills. The English struggle with everything but field sports and cricket. Don't even bother to try and reproduce that superb dish from Paris. Be content that the following recipe will get you close.

Ingredients

1 piece fine raw steak
3 potatoes
1 tsp Worcestershire sauce
1 sprig thyme or rosemary
1 sprig tarragon
Olive oil, butter, salt & pepper

Accompaniments

Burgundy
Gramophone record of 'April in Paris'

Instead of attempting to create 'pommes frites', settle for round slices of potatoes fried in delicious steak juices

Cooking

Rub steak with salt. Peel, quarter and boil potatoes until just cooked. While potatoes are boiling, combine chopped tarragon with some hot melted butter and pepper, and chill the mixture in refrigerator. Drain potatoes and reserve. Coat salted steak with olive oil and fry in hot pan. Add Worcestershire sauce, sprig of thyme or rosemary and large knob butter to pan. Spoon liquid over steak while cooking (approximately 2 minutes either side depending on size and thickness of meat). Remove steak and fry the potatoes in steak juices until golden brown. Serve steak with potatoes and pat of tarragon butter.

27

Introduction

A tavern dish, attributed to the Welsh, of unknown etymological origin, allows the deployment of cheese as a main course, disrupting the traditional sequence whereby cheese is served after soup, fish, meat and dessert. Combine cheese with fish in the recipe and the sequence is completely bust. Never mind. Treat the dish for the delicacy it is, a gastronomic pearl for consumption when time disallows the formal sequence of dining. We can see you arching your eyebrows at the prospect of re-acquaintance with smoked haddock, ruined in school kitchens by cooks dedicated to the gastronomic misery of the young gentlemen in their care, presented to the unfortunate victims as salty yellow lumps submerged in a tasteless milky fluid thick with sharp bones. You will recall the cries of 'Please sir, Simkins minor has turned blue again' as yet another boy is carried from the dining hall to matron.

However, you are old enough now to handle smoked haddock without risk to your person, and the fish in question is not far behind Dover sole in the list of the world's great seafoods, the smoked version possessing a piquancy which deserves attention by persons of discernment such as yourself.

*Smoked haddock
on ciabatta toast
with grilled cheese
and water cress*

Notes

Smoked Haddock Rarebit

Simkins minor, recovered from the incident with the fish bone, fielding at fine leg

Ingredients

2 small smoked haddock fillets
100g mature cheddar, grated
1 tsp wholegrain mustard
1 tbsp Worcestershire sauce

1 egg
1 sprig water cress
25g butter
1 large ciabatta roll

Cooking

Poach haddock fillets in pan of simmering water for 5 minutes. Allow to cool, remove any skin, search carefully for bones, very carefully, remove and pat fillets dry with kitchen paper. Mix cheese, mustard, Worcestershire sauce and egg in a bowl. Slice ciabatta roll into two halves, butter the surfaces and cover with small layer water cress. Lay the smoked haddock pieces onto the bed of watercress and apply the cheese mixture over the fish. Grill until golden and bubbling. Decorate with more water cress.

Where sheep may safely graze, not so much the lambs

Notes

_____

_____

_____

_____

_____

_____

_____

WARNING

This dish should only be attempted by
gentlemen sober enough to transfer the hot
roasting pan from the oven to a heat-resistant
kitchen surface safely

Roast Lamb

The trick is to elevate the joint on pads of onions

Ingredients

1 leg lamb
1 large onion
2 large potatoes
1 sprig rosemary
Olive oil, salt & pepper

For gravy:
1 tbsp flour
50g butter
1 glass port

Accompaniments

Mint jelly
Vegetables of choice

Cooking

Preheat oven to 240°C (220°C fan). Peel and slice onion into 4 pads of equal width. Rub lamb with olive oil, salt and pepper. Place lamb on pads of onion in roasting pan. Add rosemary and 3 tbsp olive oil to base of pan, and place pan in centre of oven. Slice potatoes into 4 halves and par-boil for 10 minutes. Take deep breath, open oven door and carefully insert potatoes into pan. 30 minutes later, take deep breath, open oven door and rotate potatoes.

When lamb is cooked (approximately 60 minutes total depending on size) remove pan from oven (see warning opposite). Transfer lamb and roast potatoes to carving dish, and dispose of rosemary sprig. Place roasting pan on cooking stove. Sprinkle flour over onions and cooking juices, add butter and port. Apply heat and stir mixture, add small amount boiling water to achieve required consistency while squashing the onions into the delicious thick dark brown gravy.

Recollection

There you were, sitting in a canvas chair outside your tent as the sun dropped beyond the distant peaks, despatched by the ambassador to report on rumours that the Chinese were building an airfield in the jungle, doodling in your sketchpad whilst your bearer made preparations for dinner, when suddenly the sound of drums drifted through the undergrowth. Nonchalantly you laid down the sketchpad. Moments later half a dozen warriors from a local tribe burst into the clearing waving spears. "What's that smell?" they demanded. "Mustard cream sauce," you replied, "made with ingredients from Fortnum's." Then turning to your bearer you said "Thomas, there will be seven for dinner."

Pork chop with mustard cream sauce

Notes

Pork Chops

That old sketch of Thomas, the bearer, preparing dinner . .

Ingredients

2 pork chops
1 tbsp butter
1 shallot or small onion
1 sprig thyme
1 bay leaf
3 tbsp brandy

2 tbsp dijon mustard
2/3 cup cream
1 1/2 tsp lemon juice
Salt, pepper, and sugar to taste
Chopped parsley to garnish

Cooking

Sear the pork chops for 2 minutes per side then turn down the heat and fry gently while you make the sauce. Chop the shallot finely. In a small saucepan melt butter over medium heat. Add shallot and sauté until translucent. Add brandy (turn off heat briefly), mustard, cream, thyme and bay leaf. Simmer to cook-off the alcohol and until the sauce reduces slightly. Finally stir in the lemon juice. Taste and season with salt, pepper, and just a little sugar as needed. Remove the pork from frying pan when blood no longer flows from knife incision. Allow to rest for 10 minutes on a cutting board. Serve with sauce spooned over the pork chop and garnished with parsley.

Introduction

In your father's time in the plains of India the locals shot grouse off the telegraph wires and served them in the officers' mess. While scavenging in your larder for something to eat, you encounter the leftovers of roast grouse from that dinner party earlier in the week, the one before the house emptied and you were left alone in disgrace. Why not recreate that dish your father used to enjoy, you say to yourself? The trouble is, you don't know how to make curry. Never mind. Just follow the instructions opposite, applicable equally to the leftovers of pheasant, partridge and other game birds, and you will be transported to the plains of India.

They shot them off the telegraph wires . . .

𝔑otes

Curried Grouse

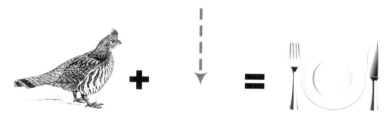

Preparations

Telephone the nearest Indian restaurant, explain the situation and seek advice. There is no need to shout. Staff in Indian restaurants speak English competently nowadays and will understand your requirements. While awaiting delivery of the dishes from the restaurant, strip the meat from the grouse and place a bottle of gin in freezer.

Cooking

Heat the leftovers of grouse in a pan with some butter. Stir into one of the Indian sauces on receipt. Commence the feast, accompanied by sips of gin with lemon and iced water.

Introduction

A long established favourite, served in the taverns of England from Shakespearian times and beyond, steak and kidney pie is one of the simplest dishes to prepare requiring only the ability to combine certain basic ingredients into a pie dish, cover with a layer of puff pastry, and transport to and from the oven without the need for medical treatment.

Fresh from the Middle Ages

𝔑otes

WARNING

The pie dish will be extremely hot after cooking.
Wear oven gloves. Check first for holes, then
ensure fingers of gloves haven't been removed
by your daughter to make puppets

Steak & Kidney Pie

Ingredients

500g fresh steak and kidney mixture
50g butter
1 large onion
1 tbsp Worcestershire sauce
2 tbsp flour

1 cup sliced mushrooms
1 cup red wine
1 sprig thyme
1 packet frozen puff pastry
Olive oil, salt and pepper

Accompaniments

Guinness, Brown Ale or Burgundy
Vegetables of choice

Cooking

Pre-heat oven to 220°C (200°C fan). Slice the onions, fry in olive oil until golden, add steak and kidneys with butter and braise the mixture. Stir flour into wine and pour into pie dish. Add mushrooms, Worcestershire sauce, thyme and contents of frying pan. Stir mixture, insert finger, taste and season with salt and pepper as required. Roll out thin layer of puff pastry, Cover pie dish with pastry and cook in oven for 15 minutes or until pastry is golden brown.

Introduction

From time to time you think fondly of those days long ago when, for some trifling offence, the enhancement of your prayer book with unflattering sketches of the vicar, for example, you were despatched to your room without supper, to be saved by the cook who smuggled to the nursery a plate of spam fritters, some buttered bread and a glass of milk. The taste lingers contentedly in your memory. It would never do to be seen eating such menial fare these days but, now that you are alone, without staff, awaiting the arrival of divorce papers. why not turn the clock back? Fritters are easy to prepare. You can dispense with the bread and butter. Instead, how about some fresh asparagus to elevate the status of the meal? Or why not be done with convention and accompany the spam with some of your daughter's baked beans? Better keep quiet about the beans, though. Word travels swiftly around the county. You don't want people muttering that standards have dropped at your estate.

Spam fritters

𝕹otes

𝔑urserp 𝔓latter

Ingredients

1 can spam
1 can baked beans
2 tbsp flour
1 egg

½ cup milk
25g butter
Olive oil, salt and pepper

Cooking

In a mixing dish create a volcano of flour. Crack egg and deposit contents into volcano. Mix egg and flour with fork, gradually adding milk until the batter is consistency of thick cream. Heat olive oil in frying pan. Open can of spam, slice meat thickly. Clasping each slice with tongs, dip both sides in batter and fry. In separate pan heat baked beans with plenty of butter and pepper. If you are sure nobody is looking, consume the platter with a glass of milk.

"If that doesn't sink you, we'll load the guns with spotted dick."

Notes

_____

_____

_____

_____

_____

_____

Caution

The cooking process involves the use of string and boiling water.
You may need a member of the gardening staff in attendance, to
tie the string and, if you've had a glass or two, hold you steady
while you lower/raise the basin into/from the boiling water.

Spotted Dick

Spotted Dick is the naval version of syrup sponge pudding, supplemented with currants, suet and rum which gives the dish its spicy flavour. Served with generous volumes of cream the dish's arrival in country house dining halls is greeted with alarm by females anxious of their figures, and with enthusiastic applause by gentlemen of all shapes and incomes.

Moist, crumbly, piquant . . .

Ingredients

300g plain flour
2 tsp baking powder
150g shredded suet
75g caster sugar
110g currants

1 tsp nutmeg, grated
1 lemon, zest only
200ml milk
2 tbsp rum
butter, for greasing

Cooking

Place the flour, baking powder, shredded suet, caster sugar, currants and lemon zest into a bowl and mix to combine. Add the milk and rum, and stir to make a soft dough. Grease a pudding basin with butter and spoon the mixture into the basin. Cover with a piece of folded greaseproof paper. Tie around the edge with string to secure the paper and place a damp tea towel over the top. Tie once more with string to secure the tea towel. Place the basin into a large lidded saucepan and fill the pan two-thirds of the way up with water. Cover with the lid, bring to a boil and simmer for one hour.

Reunion

She's back ! Laden with parcels she embraces you and explains she had lost her mobile telephone. How stupid of me to have given cook the week off when I went shopping in town, you know how time flies in London and, yes, I spent the night with Maude, how did you get on by yourself, all alone, my poor darling, she says? "Alright, I suppose," you reply stiffly, feigning moderate indignation at the simultaneous absence of wife and kitchen staff though relieved that your manifold indiscretions appear to have been forgiven or remain undetected. When Georgina (your daughter) gets back from school tomorrow we can decorate the Christmas tree, incidentally why is your mouth covered in caster sugar, says your wife? "I've been eating mince pies," you explain.

*A year-round favourite of the well-bred though
mysteriously only available in shops at Christmas*

Notes

Mince Pies

Preparations

Long ago mince meat did indeed include meat, along with brandy and assorted fruits and spices. The meat has now gone, simplifying the recipe, which is still far too complicated for you to handle so search the deep freezer for the stock of mince pies which cook promised to maintain for you on the basis of your strongly expressed opinion that mince pies and spotted dick were the only puddings worth having.

Cooking

Heat mince pies in microwave and consume with immense amounts of cream.

Red, white or pink – dry or sweet –
wine is the natural partner of cheese

Notes

Cheeses

Finale

And so, with order restored to your household, we conclude by paying homage to the most versatile of farm products, cheese. Two countries in particular stand out, France and England. Between them their cheeses have won more awards than all other countries combined. We salute especially the soft ones of France, exemplified by Reblochon from the hills of Haute-Savoie, and the blue ones of England, exemplified by Stilton, regarded by most experts as the finest of them all.

On this theme, it is worth pointing out that the majority of dishes in this publication not only originate from the British Isles, but feature regularly in the world's best restaurants. So much for the scorn traditionally heaped upon our native fare. When next you find yourself alone, the innocent victim of fate or transparently guilty of behaviour unbecoming of a person of your stature, which with hindsight in the sober light of day you regret but which seemed amusing at the time, you wander hungrily into the kitchen clutching a copy of this publication, be comforted in the knowledge that the subjects of the recipes herein, the native foodstuffs of these islands, are quite unmatched in quality when measured against the products of other nations.

Reblochon

Wait until the cheese begins to run before eating. Do not refrigerate when ripe, keep in the larder covered with moist cloth. Do not place in container or wrap in plastic.

Stilton

Unlike soft cheeses, Stilton should be stored in airtight container in refrigerator or larder after opening, where it will continue to mature and develop its mellow creamy flavour.

45

Acknowledgements

During our researches to ensure that the recipes herein were simple enough for gentlemen unaccustomed to kitchen activities we referenced hundreds of sources, mostly in the internet, to whom we extend our thanks with assurances that we have not knowingly purloined original material from contemporary experts, choosing instead to treat old established recipes as the basis for our selections.

Every effort has been made to avoid copyright infringements, by tracing the sources of the artwork used in the text and, where applicable, by obtaining the appropriate permissions and licences.

A Gentleman's Guide to Cooking
Part 3
A Gentleman's Guide to Women, Commoners & Cooking

Old English Press

Other Books by
Old English Press

Old English Press will be publishing the following books through
Amazon during 2021 in Kindle and paperback versions.

No Barking Please
A Gentleman's Guide to Cooking
Royal Podium
The Quince River Parchment
Peter the Perpendicular (reissue)
The Escape of MV Duchess
Dangerous Flotilla

For details of the books visit the publisher's website
www.oldenglishpress.co.uk